Songs of Shaman

Calling of creation through the eyes of
Shaman

Jhanvi Mahalwal

BookLeaf
Publishing

India | USA | UK

Made with ❤ on the BookLeaf Publishing Platform
www.bookleafpub.in
www.bookleafpub.com

I am dedicating my work in honor of the Creator of the Worlds who crafted everything with so much love. Yet, we couldn't take care of his creation. He entrusted us with the safety of every being and all that resides on earth and we simply looted everything.

Acknowledgement

I wish to thank the Almighty God for helping me pen down my conscious thoughts and ushering me with the courage to pass them on to the present generation. I also wish to thank BookLeaf Publishing for popping up at the right time.

Love and Gratitude

Preface

I am not a seasoned writer, a poetess or even a shaman for that matter. I am just a speck of dust roaming through the many multiverses, which has lost its way to home like every other speck of dust that exists. Never felt at home on this planet yet the deplorable condition that its momentary inhabitants have made needs a voice. I will not try to wake up anybody but through the eyes of a shaman will try to show what the earth feels, what other beings and elements wish to convey to humans.

The collection of poems in this book is a silent cry and a voiceless outroar for help that the earth is asking from humans.

I wish my readers to visit the earth, its elements, and many other beings that exist alongside them through the eyes that keep watch over everyone and will make you accountable when the time comes!

Have a conscious reading!

Song of the Death

Sitting depressed
Utterly repressed
About to plunge from the cliff of a mental
hive
I heard a pitching voice from above the sky
A humongous hawk gawking so high
Diving into the deep ocean, I thought he died.
Inspired by the instance, I plunged with a
roaring cry.
Thud!
I thought I died
But I was soaring high
In the clutches of a griffin
Ascending and leaping towards the sky.
I inquired his congruity
peering into the mirrors of his eyes
Flap!

He opened his wings
Merged me in his furculum
And together we ascended on the cliff of life.
The world seems different with a different
vibe
I am no one's
And
No one is mine
I smiled and shot!
Dashed into the heavens up high!

Song of the Jungle

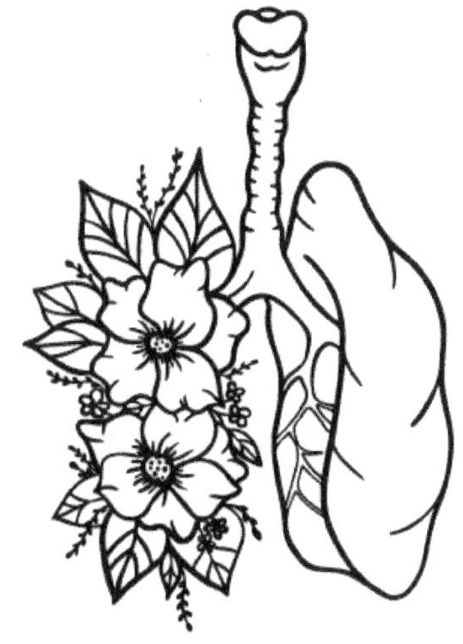

In the depths of the night, I heard a mystical
song
I leapt to focus on the lyrics to where it
belongs
I tried, I tried but the words were vague
My heart panicked as the music was awake
I cried, I cried, oh let me hear
Embrace the pain, a whiff in my ear
For let me test the grit if you can bear.
I saw a woman sitting in the woods
Playing mystical notes on her flute
All wrinkled yet at the prime of her youth.

I danced like a water dragon at her command
Leisurely melting in the river of life so
unplanned
I swam; I drifted wherever I could,
I unfurled, I merged my veins in the life's
mighty hood
I can hear the earth breathing in my lungs
I felt the lava melting in my belly's hung
Am I becoming an earth-traumatic?
Or did I feel her heart in such ecstatic
Heal me, oh zeal me
But don't peel me
I cried from the womb of the river of life
I saw the woman grinning at my deplorable
sight
She danced in enigma, I can hear her lyrics
thou,
"I am the jungle and the jungle is in you
now!"

Song of Ecstasy

Humans perceive color
At the gradient of the horizon
Creatures acknowledge grayscale
At the nature's provision
Is it day and night or nature's vision of a love
affair?
Or is it the modern man and woman coupled
in there
Day and night chase, burning themselves
Only to meet each other at the gates of hell
Thawing their souls every day in each other
Only to drift apart in the world of nether
But when they meet in the moment of enigma
Even the gods witness their bewildering,
erotic magma

And then their two worlds fall apart—
One in light and other in pitch dark
Promising to meet again, this is how they part
Incessant to meet again and fall apart.

Song of Life

In the ocean of creation, all beings are churned
Through the diasporas of construction and destruction
This is what they have earned!
Yet a dispute burning so bright
In the heart of the mighty mountain and man alike
Mountain surrenders to the mood swings of nature
While Man endeavors to change her stature

Nature is unforgiving, destructive, ruthless
and obdurate
Whenever she is in love, she is bound to
procreate
Still the audacity man chooses to show
Kneading fragile emotions in a generational
row
Knowing that she will trample once and for
all
Whatever man created, when it starts taking
toll
Noble is the mountain he knows how to bow
While man in the jaws of time chewed up so
slow
Life is but a mythical bubble—
Whatever is created will soon turn to rubble
Astute is the mountain going with the flow
Living the life every day, letting all things
grow
Look at the ambitious man, ignorant and
dense
Giving up on life at the materials' defense

Song of Aurora

I am the creation holding hues of green,
white, and pink
As the creator poured his heart through his
vibrant inks
All are amused, all are dazed
Seeing expressions so unfazed
Humans flock through every corner and nook
To gaze, admire, leaving all their hooks
I am the pride of the northern lights
But I am alone yet all alive
Advent of harsh season, planet dims its lights
Humans run back to attach themselves

To their previous lives
They treat me as a fleeting moment
Making memories underneath my sky
I cried all night and asked the Lord
"Why does all leave me alone after enjoying a
good time?"
The Lord said, "Perhaps you never noticed
your own loving sky."

Song of Ocean

Come to my deep, dark embrace
As I long for you
I am standing at the shores
I passed millenniums for you
Come! Let me take you away from this
material world
Come! Let's play in my cold, aqueous riddle
In your longing, oh my beloved
I have destroyed many homes
I ransacked, plundered, and destroyed many
vessels
You can't resist me for long
I will make you pay half of the labor—
Your lungs will sing a foamy song.
I wish to feel your muffled breaths in my
tight embrace

I crave to see you floating dead in my depths'
solace
I will feed you to all my creatures that lie low
Remnants of you are welcome for wild weeds
to grow
I will make you taste the plastic
Which is a result of ignorance so drastic
I will merge your soul into mine
Shaking you out of the prison so fine
Why crave the sunlight's portal?
It's your time to become immortal

Song of the Night

I welcome in my stir, you the children of
night
As I see you fading away from the warmth of
light
You make me believe that you long for me
Just like the old days
When the monsters took the stride
You love me so bad
I will give you soul-screeching unease
I will make love to you
When I push you into the darkest crease
I will kiss you so hard
Pouring in your consciousness the
bewildering dis-ease

I will destroy all your fears
Unleashing storm in eyes full of tears
I am no Christ as I love to bite
Your hopeless, regretful sight
I promise you a never-ending love
With deep depression in your hub
Crucifying your soul's sanity
I will love you right
All night!

Song of Day

Do you feel blessed at the sight of light?
Walking through my lanes, beaming so right
You hustle, you bustle all along the day
You pray, you play in my soothing alley
I am your friend, walking hand in hand
Through thick and thin across this land
But you betray me at the sight of night
Hurting my feelings holy and bright
Still I forgive you like all days
Calling you to play under the sun's rays
Come, let's play in the sunflower fields
Come, let's sit under the shade of trees
Come, let's run in the breezy ease
But you crave the insomniac world

Dying to kiss the mysterious skull
Why don't you get up, smile and shine?
Tossing in bed you always whine
Count your days as they are less
Once it's over you will pay the cess

Song of Love

Some say that love is God
Others say it is the heart's abode
On the human dimension it is wrongly
treasured
This is how the Shaman had it measured
Seeking God or seeking pleasure
Heart has become a thing of leisure
Dirty tricks and manipulation ever
In name of love, getting physical forever
Then what is love? O Shaman you reveal
But don't you dare play devil's deal

Love is not ecstasy, not even romance
Dwelling in sexual desires, you don't get a
chance
Love is pure, love is peace
Search within yourself, you will find it with
ease
Looking for someone as a soul mate
Physical world is just a checkmate
Wrongly lured to the twin flames' path
It doesn't exist as I did the math
Settle the murky waters of your soul
Try reading in it the divine, lost scroll
You will encounter a scared little child
Sitting in the shadows, running from the wild
Hug him tight, make him bright
Try pulling him out in the holy light
Love is all around and love is you
You will realize what was long due
Pour from your cup into the earth's spirit
She is the lover you forgot to visit
The more you pour, the more you get
The lover and love you will never regret.

Song of Hate

I am hate, a product of love
That betrayal ate
I am hate, burning, longing, and seething
with anger
Jealousy, pain at the hell's gate
I am hate, once desired, now replaced!
I am hate, the glorious days
Shunned through the narcissistic ways
I am hate, standing in a corner, dejected,
repealed,
In an obnoxious dismay
I am hate, depressed, staggering, hollow, void,
Chained, suffocating, in mental distress
I am hate, self-sabotaging, self-incriminating,
Self-intimidating, and self-suppressed!

I am hate, boundless, mayhem, unruly, errant,
And badly behaved
I am hate, I suffer a lot, pleading for help
Begging guilty, expecting to be exonerated!
I am hate, I beg for one chance, don't shun,
don't replace.
I am hate, I kill innocent
I dance berserk in others' grace!

Song of Devotion

A coward kneels at the altar of Supreme
Scared, greedy, and unsure of the Creator's
potential in him
It begs, and begs, and begs some more
Demanding God to do its filthy chores
The Creator is in utter dismay, shocked at his
craft
"This is what I made!"
Lucifer laughs from the depths of hell
"For this, O Father you cast me from my
shell!"
The Father, who arts in heaven, what have you
made!
This creature is worse than a demon
Yet seeks a heavenly upgrade!
You say he is devoted to your mercy
I say he is playing a manipulative derby
Were you just not happy with us?
That you crafted on earth this selfish ruckus!

Song of Birds

I am twice-born, wisest of all
I dash towards the sky and never fall
I trust my wings O human weaklings
I can build my nest wherever I stall
Just like you, I breathe out of an egg
But you are the one carrying an emotional
bag
Appearance of mine is a bit twisted
Not like the roads straight
But I am not a believer of fables
Hanging on the devotional gates
You are the most intelligent and smart
But what have you gained?
You were born free yet seem stuck and
chained

I trust my wings, instincts and one God
While you exist under the shade of fear's nod
I come; I go, whether fast or slow
But you repeat life in the same row.

Song of Earth

Am I the maiden, mother or crone
Or the molten metal
Bubbling in my belly's cauldron
Am I the season, harsh and soft
Or the drought, famine, or harvest's loft
All you come here for a momentary rest
At my pleasure! Be my guest!
I am full of fury and sometimes love
Or the toughest demon or just a pure dove
Am I breathing? Do I have a heart?
Yes! The lungs are choking, jokes apart
Am I patient, am I haste
Inviting you here is such a waste
You plundered my bounties, mutilated my
home
I wonder about the halting moment
Of your false throne!

Song of Butterfly

My life is a mystery, a dilemma, a puzzle
I thought I died in my cocoon's muzzle
I lost all hope under the suffocating ruffle
Life poured nectar and made me guzzle
With a gentle stroke, I bid goodbye to the
fading fizzle
All complimented my beauty now that I
dance and dazzle
Yet the same mystery, a dilemma, a puzzle
In the cocoon or the moments of grapple
I am the same soul, why now such a sizzle?
The world is blind to the venom they drizzle
Ignoring the truth for the lies they chisel.

Song of Trees

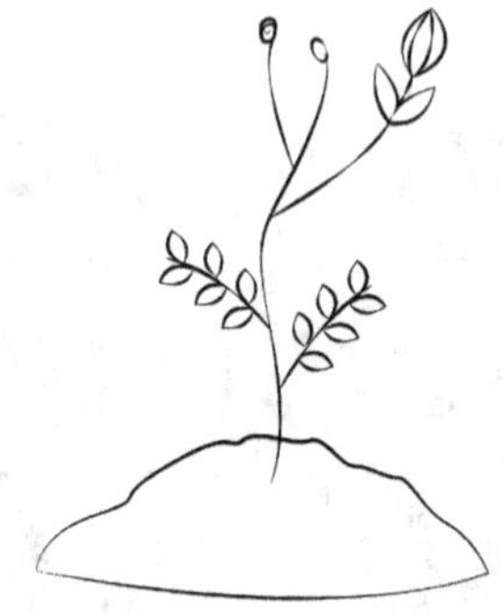

A saint, meditating, embedded in the earth
Like the mighty mountains devoid of dearth
Under my shelter you got what you want
I even gave you the rosary for the holy name
you chant
For you to prosper,
I crossed continents and spread
But you, O traitor, felled me because my
blood is not red!
I am your lifeline
Your friend in despair
But you preferred, over me
My flesh, made into table and chair!
A day will come when the sun will burn all
Earth will agonize for breath
Like a dead leaf, all beings will fall!

But then, O my friend, it will be too late
As my days will be over on earth
I will witness you too annihilate.

Song of Human

I am the Supreme, I am the King
All bow down
You heard a bell ring
For me, my Lord kicked Lucifer out
He bestowed all earth to me
I need a shout-out
He made me the lord of every being
I guess I am his special
I did the counting
The Lord is so merciful, he forgives all I do
Whether I break his heart
Or subject his creation to screw
Stories of hell and heaven are so fake

It's a crafty mess—did Christ die for my sake!
Now I am immune to all ordeals
I can ask the devil in the eye, what's his deal!
I am the devil of the devil
The world can see
Unleashing the wrath, pushing humanity to
flee
Silently, death's nook drags me out.
Whispering in my ear,
Do you need a shout-out?

Song of God

All pervading, omniscience,
omnibenevolence, omnipotence
The one you kill for, by holy books' every
stance
I am this and I am that
Yet choose to dwell in your neglecting hearts
I love you so much that I couldn't stay apart
For you, O my creation, I took all the darts
I don't want an altar, candle, flower or
sacrifice
I just want your attention, that will suffice
For you, O' my creation, I stepped down from
my throne
I tried touching your heart
Alas! It is made of stone!

I wonder who refurbished my holy seat
I wonder who planned this cunning deceit
I came here to soften your heart
In the garb of prophets, Rama, Krishna, a feet
apart
You are still deep asleep
In the embrace of death's leap
It's time that I leave you at your own feet,
For the past and tragedy to repeat
Ending creation is the only choice
What I created, I couldn't rejoice!

Song of Darkness & Light

A forever fight ensued between Darkness and
Light
Solving the eternal question, who is wrong
and who is right!
From heaven to earth playing with humans
day and night
Proving only one point
Who amidst them is bestowed with the
shining armor,
And who amongst them is that brave knight?
What a holy question, the answer lies in
earth's deplorable sight
"If you both save humanity, I will declare the
winner
Do you have the might?"

Asked the earth with all hopes bright
Darkness and Light were shrouded in silence
As they were responsible for humanity's
plight
Making them pawns, luring them through
insane dreams' flight
Asked the earth – "Did you do right?"
Leave my abode right this instant
Take your fight out of my sight!
Darkness and Light smirked at Earth so quite
"Make us leave, o' Earth! If you feel it's right!"
But now the fight is no longer between black
and white
It has taken a toll and reached its height
Dare you challenge us; we will show you a war
ignite
For the humans you beg—what a despising
sight!
Stay in the corner, bow down and be polite
The humans you speak of, we stepped here at
their invite
There's no looking back now
The fight will continue forever
Between wrong and right!

Song of The End

Trumpets have been blown
All holy signs have shown
The kings will dive into war
Betting their blood and bone!
Death's jaw is opening wide
Can you hear its hungry tone?
Half the world is rushing for power
Half seems to be hooked on their phone
Acting so naïve, rolling in dreams
Remaining world seeking pleasure in money
and moan
Cities bombed, humanity raped!
When did the seed of hatred grow?
Trying to correct with tiny hope
Centuries have passed, time has flown

Scriptures are right, humanity is dead
World is approaching the end zone
But this time, there will be no ark of Noah
You are prophesied to die alone
You the man of science and power
You can never change what's set in stone!
Trumpets have been blown
All holy signs have shown.

Song of Witches' Cauldron

Stir, stir in the cauldron it goes
Bubble, bubble as the world lay dozed
Hush, hush as the witch boils the brew
Ego, one portion; ignorance, two
Cruelty in base with fakeness and shrew
One spoonful greed, with cry and hue
All set with the potion, purple and blue
Gulp, gulp, O' newborn, the potion through
Bewitched by the pentagram that illusion
drew
Lust, lust, O young men, the sins that grew
Damned by attachment and arrogance that
flew

Die, die, O old men chained with hell's crew
Beware of the cauldron that's cooking your
stew!

Song Of Shaman

In the dark moonless nights
I often hear the hoary cries
Is it a warning, is it a pain
Or a challenge to dance in the murky rain
She is the medicine flowing through the veins
Is she the mother willingly chained?
I knelt to touch the thumping ground
Only to find her heart's pumping sound
Yes, she's alive! Yes, she's here
Beating nature's drum everywhere
She called my name from the rainy woods
I dashed to her wearing a shaman's hood
I looked for her, for any trace
I stood alone in the darkest embrace
I doubt I heard a cry for help

Or was it a lone wolf's wailing yelp!
Mother, O Mother where are you now?
She whispered through the seeds that were
sown
I am here, I am now!
You lost me in the future's bow
I am breaking chains and taking vow
Destruction of all, I now bestow!

Song of Nectar

Once upon a time when darkness veiled the
skies
Gods and demons, with ambitions in their
eyes
Planned a combat holding their warring rods
Warcrafts were assembled with permission of
the lord!
Who will get the nectar? What are the odds?
Churn! Churn! The ocean, you have the
trinities' nod
Vishnu to Shiva favored the righteous in the
line
They all pre-decided to make their future
shine

One drank the poison, the other bewitched
them all
The entire creation favored, where the trinity
took the call
Allegations of deceit and favor were plastered
everywhere
But why were the humans ignored in the
battle for nectar share!

Song of Magical Clay

One fine day when God wanted to play
He picked a pile of clay, turned his magic
wand to sway
He modeled many beings
But his favorite was despised by the creature
with the wings
Comparisons were drawn
Heated arguments from dusk to dawn
A bet was placed, and the favorite turned into
a pawn
Heavenly beings will throng, singing destiny's
song
The pawn will dance to the righteous beats
If not, hell waits for his beats gone wrong!
For a good deed, a heaven
For a bad one, a hell!
Winged beings mocked his life
Keeping him in a mental cell

The purpose is defeated, to craft the pawn
He has become a weary rug in Eden's lawn
Did somebody ask, what's in the heart of the
pawn?
Who cares for him, said an angel with a yawn
The Creator seems busy in other worldly
affairs
Did he abandon him in the illusory snare?

Song of Blood

In the hush of the twilight's breath
Where the shadows dance and spirits tread
I hear through the veins of Mother Earth
A song of blood where life is wed
With every beat, the ancestors call
Whispers woven in the wind's soft sigh,
Their stories flow through veins of living,
In the sacred circle, where the lost do not die
Red rivers run through the heart of the forest,
Each drop a memory, each drop a tale,
Of warriors bold and lovers parted,
Of joy and sorrow, of triumph and wail
I stand upon the edge of the world,

With my drum as my heart, my voice as my
guide,
Calling forth spirits from the depths of the
night,
To dance in the fire where shadows abide
Oh, blood of the earth, oh, blood of my kin,
You pulse in the roots of each tree that I see,
In the howl of the wolf and the cry of the
hawk,
In the silence that follows when the wild
winds flee.
Let me weave your essence into my song,
As I journey through realms where the lost
souls roam,
For every life lived is a thread in this tapestry,
A reminder that we are never alone!

Song of Magic

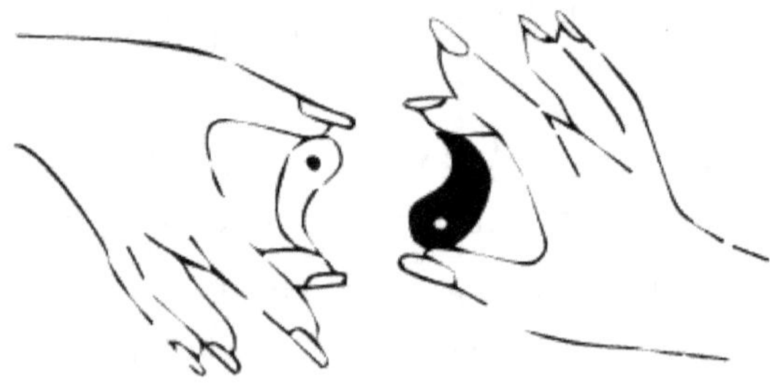

In the stillness of the twilight hour,
Where the veil is thin and shadows bloom,
I gather the whispers of ancient boughs,
And weave them into a drapery of loom.
Oh, spirits of the earth, of sky and sea,
Grant me your power, your wisdom so deep,
With every breath, I call forth your magic,
Awake from your slumber, rise from your
sleep.
The wind carries secrets, the fire holds
dreams,
In the dance of the flames, I see visions
unfold,
Each flicker a story, each spark a desire,
In the warmth of the hearth, new tales to be
told

With herbs in my pouch and stones in my
hand,
I summon the elements, both fierce and
divine,
Water's soft flow and earth's sturdy embrace,
Air's gentle whisper and fire's fierce shine.
Oh, magic of moonlight, silver and bright,
Guide my intentions as stars start to gleam,
In the circle I draw, with salt and sage,
I open the doorway to realms beyond dream.
Let the spirits of ancestors gather around,
Their voices like echoes in the cool evening
air,
With every heartbeat, I feel their presence,
In this sacred communion, I find solace and
care.

I chant for the healing of body and soul,
For courage to rise when the shadows grow
long,
In the rhythm of nature, I find my own pulse,
In the song of magic, I am ever strong.
Oh, dance of the cosmos, weave through my
veins,

As I journey through realms where the unseen
reside,
With each step I take on this path of the
mystic,
I embrace the enchantment that flows deep
inside.
So come forth, dear spirits, let your magic
ignite,
In the heart of this shaman, let our souls
intertwine,
For in every incantation and every soft prayer,
The song of magic is eternal—divine.